JEFFREY WAINWRIGHT was born in Stoke-on-Trent in 1944 and was educated locally and at the University of Leeds. He has taught at the University of Wales, Long Island University in Brooklyn and for many years at the Manchester Metropolitan University where he was Professor in the Department of English and its Writing School until 2008.

His first poetry collection was published by Northern House in 1971 and first full book, *Heart's Desire*, by Carcanet in 1978. Carcanet Press also publish his *Selected Poems* (1985), *The Red-Headed Pupil* (1994), *Out of the Air* (1999) and *Clarity or Death!* (2008). He has translated plays by Péguy, Claudel and Corneille for BBC Radio 3 and his version of Bernard-Marie Koltès' *In the Silence of Cotton Fields* was broadcast in March 1999. The play has subsequently been performed by the Actors Touring Company and published by Methuen.

Jeffrey Wainwright has published widely on poetry, including *Poetry: The Basics* (Routledge 2004) and his book on the poetry of Geoffrey Hill, *Acceptable Words* (Manchester University Press, 2005).

Also by Jeffrey Wainwright from Carcanet Press

Heart's Desire
Selected Poems
The Red-Headed Pupil
Out of the Air
Clarity or Death!

JEFFREY WAINWRIGHT

The Reasoner

CARCANET

First published in Great Britain in 2012 by

Carcanet Press Limited
Alliance House
Cross Street
Manchester M2 7AQ

www.carcanet.co.uk

A CIP catalogue record for this book is available from the British Library

ISBN 978 1 84777 146 9

The publisher acknowledges financial assistance from Arts Council England

Supported by
ARTS COUNCIL
ENGLAND

Typeset by XL Publishing Services, Tiverton
Printed and bound in England by SRP Ltd, Exeter

Odysseus shakes his head. He has come to this borderland to question Tiresias; to learn how, if ever, he will reach his own father and home in Ithaka again. He wants to know. And this is what the dead want too. Every one of them – queens, princesses, kings of men – has asked for news. They have forgotten how hard it is for the living to know things. That the rule is one place at one time. The way they claw at him – it's as if they expect him to have been everywhere at once. The truth is he's as ignorant as they were. As they still are.

Elizabeth Cook, *Achilles* (2001)

In my profession one must know everything.

Don Quixote

Reason is a child, angered by tiredness, that will not sleep.

Helen Tookey

In Memory of
John Davidson (1939–2007), historian

1

Starting early with my dog, boundlessly,

or on a solitary walk by a riverside,

or in a stew or a studio, or in a stew in a studio
a proper brown one,

you will find me.

But am I the same in your eyes as in mine,
or in that third eye, the barber's captious glass?

My dome is as innocent, as artless, as a wig-stand;
the elastic that fastens my spectacles has crimped one ear;
I am spry still but stooped from the books I bear,
a few good bindings but glue-split paperbacks mostly,
bundled, strapped and wedged into packs, fardels,
so that philosophers laugh as I waddle by.
Also about me: pyramids, cubes and squares,
a wood-gauge and a rule, as Don Quixote says:
'in my profession
you must know everything'.

I am one who would know,
and thus be happy.

2

A single filament of a spider's web
only appears because of how
for these ten minutes the light plays it,
like the back and forth of a slide guitar
as it is caught in the vagaries
of the tiny wind.

Nothing else anywhere, ever, has these,
offers these same movements to an eye.
Hard to grasp how this thread and light as seen
is 'intellectually inferred'.

But looking at one thing am I missing another?

Beliefs are necessary, I do believe.
There is enough white water and storm scum
to show that life is not a book group
or a week in a hammock.
Not that abeyance is a crime:
it may be praiseworthy, principled even,
enabling us to hang out with whatever
and whoever we please for the while;
in some desperate circs. it might even keep us alive.
But ... but ... 'but' will butter no parsnips
in the end, and should doubt doubt doubt,
as it surely will, there is only 'and so on
and so on and so on' until, as sages keep saying,
'all I know is that I know nothing' –
I really do believe that – *oh my, do I?*
Oh yes indeed I do.

4

Is our language complete? Not on your life!
Not like H_2SO_4. Not like the law of sines
with its allowance for the ambiguous case.
But there is the hope

the *one who hopes*

for simple agreements,
perfect understanding
for nothing not ever irregular

In Stoke-on-Trent post-war we were keen on Esperanto.
Here, where breathing could be difficult,
was an inspiration to get out the door,
to world peace, nation same-speaking peace unto nation,
so charas could criss-cross from Dresden to Dresden,
Burslem to Bialystok,
happy wanderers, buying pots of tea effortlessly,
and explaining the laws of cricket faultlessly
to Russians Germans Poles and Jews,
without an itch and nary a crux word.

Is our language complete?   No way José
exclamation point. For all the rolling off the tongue
words remain such dullards, their relations obscure.

I — wish — that — she — would — call.
Just tell me, if you can, how what I mean is there.
Or even in: *I — do — wish — that — she — would — call.*
Just tell me, if you can, how what I feel is there.
How do such, or any, sentences give forth,
bring into presence, stand in for, resemble … ?
No way. But just watch them do it.

Is our language complete? Are you kidding?
Very often. Which is part of the lack.
I can't claim though that I am lied to often.
Even house-agents' clerks don't say the thing-which-is-not
deliberately, they are just optimists
by training, and the ones I know, the press they get,
it's hard not to sympathise. Would he really
leave a girl like that in her bedsit in her nothings?
Could her executive comportment turn peevish,
lead to murder in the master bedroom even?
I don't know.

Is our language complete? You bet it is!
Name one thing it can't do.
It can dawdle meaning-less-ly like this,
or be doing the same thing soul-ful-ly, if it says so,
drifting along the ramparts in a floaty dress,
the chalky hills [*enter here*] in the moonlight,
could be given anything to do,
as they were once said to skip.
The only question it has to ask itself is
how much is a sufficiency, elegant or otherwise?

Is our language complete? Well, you read the lines /
lies in the last poem, decide for yourself.
In truth I stumble and cast about even when
I'm talking to myself. There are the best of tools
in the tidiest of racks under the stairs
and these words are not among them, nor – I 'hazard' –
are there any such places words may be found.
But do not despair – and that's an order –
there are no angels, thus no perfect prattling,
and the painstaking repair of spiders' webs
best left to what's best adapted.
As the nightingale 'with her sweet self she wrangles'
we must just strive with our creature tongue.

but who can I talk to? To you?
I'm always looking for a way to talk
and I could talk to you
but who might you be?
Are you a parson and should I be afraid?
See! I feel you misunderstand already –
I don't mean these days a reverend
but someone parsonical, already guyed
by the adjective, already gagged
but still mumming in that corner of my eye
I will not turn to –
Oh, you are not my heart's delight,
you load my heart, you want me
for your adversary and that's fair enough
in a democracy, and though I know I would lose
the argument, something I really fear,
what is the most you can deal me,
what would stand me bare-headed in the market place?
I know, but with the lily-stink about me,
not in words, or otherwise, can I turn to you.

I'll take me to the *visagiste*.
She won't say, 'Mornin' Squire, how're y' diddlin'
but just set tranquilly to work so that, without a word,
I have every assurance of a new face.
My polpy, and as twilight falls, geranium-coloured nose
will be no more; my skull bones will be cracked
and blended, no longer angular;
my skin – how you say? – hydrated.
Smat! Smat! I shall be new.
I shall know who I am.

Things are not what they seem.
This is the big idea of the detective story,
as of Plato. What is really happening as
I study his palm is that the conjuror
has taken my braces and my watch.
There is always a second world
and it's not even out there,
we're just watching the wrong thing.

But in the worst of mysteries there are no clues,
or, if you *must* believe in them, they cannot be read.
Who took my braces, my watch, the lost children may,
the authorities say, never be known,
save in the parallel and smug universe of crimes.

No, not suddenly; gradually, bit by bit,
and reluctantly, after much valiant struggle,
one recognises the disorder:
one cupboard, cabinet or tallboy will not do,
place mats are never in their place,
nor tea towels, pillowcases, serviettes;
the crucial kitchen-drawer always has
the wrong batteries, withered elastic bands,
part-warranties, a fuse, sundry string (some plasticated),
a dead pen-torch and none of it helps,
despite planning,
none of it helps –
objects that survive, survive,
like this stout black box 12 inches × 6 × 6.
One must never admit it is all one has.

Hotshit philosopher, just tell me *what*
is always veiled, or, at least, you know, the *kind* of thing?
or what on earth are all our interpretations
of?
I'm guessing I'm not to expect
a silver ladder from the parted clouds,
nor a window to open
and she let down her hair.
These are the beautiful stories of revelation and release
and are ruled out.
Yes, in fairness, I know you know
that fewer even of you yourselves
can, or would want to turn your heads towards
– crudely put, but how else? – the truth,
and return to tell us just how things are
and thus should be

– fiercer yet burns the fire,
the shadows ever more spectacular
and Virtue no longer tries to peep
but foxtrots, jogs or saunters in the flames.

He'd been waiting for a taxi, Pamuk says.
He had got home at last, and just as he put his key in the lock
he concluded that any meaning anyone might find in the world
he found by chance.

I'm not happy with this.
If the only meaning comes by chance
is chance the only meaning?
But understanding taxis and understanding birds,
earthworms or foxgloves,
following the methods each for each,
might reveal the same algorithm eventually,
and each algorithm slot into the next,
ever outwards until we have some such triumphal cry as
'l'amor che move il sole e l'altre stelle!'
and, before you laugh, if one thing is to move
heaven and earth might it not best be love?
There is a voracity for laws which I know I feel,
just like the man approaching his own front door,
I would conclude, conclude.

15

The beauty outside constantly interrupts.

George Seferis, *Journal*

These black-eyed, snow-white pansies for instance,
careless of their opulence,
generous little souls,
and the raucous lorikeets, green and red,
in the trees near the ocean,
and the ocean and the ocean of light they live in.

I could cultivate an indoor phrase, 'pansy-blind',
as though there is a tale to be told of them
as of every meadow, grove and stream.
Better not interrupt,
which will have to mean: be blind, be deaf,
do not push fingers out towards them.

Can it be true one ancient put his own eyes out
to see more clearly? Can we think yet?

Courtesy of Reg Mombassa
I should like to draw attention
to the part-consonance of
Calvary and *Clovelly*.

It is not immaculate, not as nice
as a parallelogram, agreed,
but does serve as a pointer
to what, in language, might sort with what,
what might tumble together
as false friends do
leaving us as under a signpost
which has been tampered with overnight
and is now trying to keep a straight face.

Which leads me to ask have you ever noticed
how the Madonna is always trying
to get some reading done?
The book is falling to the pavement
as the angel calls,
or open on her lap,
or on the lectern
with a book-box spilling over by her foot;
even later on she is still absorbed as the bambino
finds a wicked thorn to play with.

Must she have had some other life,
and, it seems to us moderns, a very modern one,
but it fell away?
Could it be said she was saved from words?

Suppose I gave up reading:
wouldn't I start to realise at last
that being genned up on the dispositions
at Caporetto, or the strange under-the-raft world
of poems, or made-up lives
in made-up towns in north Ontario,
or even the best thumbnail cribs of Socrates
are not going to profit me?
What is stock for the mind?
If we can make Nature wordless
is she then not enough?
especially if I choose just one thing to stand for her,
nothing rich like persimmon or lavender
(no sightless pansy or brash lorikeet)
but — a spade-chunk of marl perhaps,
nasturtium-yellow, glinting on its cut side
for a few moments, then lustreless, immobile,
and wormless, but something that might unload
and exalt the mind, and in this way
make it the study for a better life.

In the reading rooms for working men,
it was written:
'Get Knowledge, Get Understanding.'
But what I keep thinking is
I don't know what the mind is
other than something
that tries to keep me safe for a while,
without, it seems, being exhausted by the task.

But is the breeze my superior?
Yes the mind's a house pressed hard
between two trees, fir-like, dark,
both growing from what they do not know.
But when it thinks '[*dash*] knows'
it knows it means, *de facto*:
'It is known' and remains only to be found
and we can get on to it – hurrah! hurrah!
This is how I keep falling for Progress.

Distant percussions. Perhaps a bird-scarer,
perhaps a practised shot practising,
perhaps – though there would first be puffs of smoke –
the detonation of dead fireworks for safety's sake.

The mind can associate anything with anything
and casts about: will sounds go with sights
or movements, this wisp of thistledown going quickly by?

There is probably no end to this ingenuity,
but let's be frugal and not seek for examples.

Today, and maybe for all time, I will insist
that the percussions must also be met elsewhere,
in a space that is more than this mind.

21

To finish a swim, to come back from a walk
as the mist dissolves below,
as the fruit warms on the tree
and to turn to newspapers is,
as George Seferis says,
to rip bandages from miserable wounds.

There is life but not the same life.

Sharing air and age and books,

tap-tapping to each other, cy-dots,

but a lizard braves the sunny square
and is faster than a bird's glance to its cleft.
You stumble, one step is more than a thought.

While you wrestle the Beast hourly
I stretch out along a divan and a stool
for twenty minutes' nice shuteye.

How much of life is dancing?

How much of life is movement?

A blink for yes, two blinks for no.

Already most upright in his plastic chair,
as the musicians lift their instruments
he lifts his head and fixes the stage steadfastly.
For all we know the music may be something to do tonight,
it may be more of the noise to be endured everywhere,
it may be a gift whose moves and shapes will not numb
but release his mind. For all we know –
that is to say, 'however much we know',
dismissing what we know not as immaterial
but as not sufficient.
Living next to widowhood we are onlookers only.

Some simple sights for some states of mind
must be cruel. For the bereaved,
threads of all kinds must tear at the heart –
the wind rips the spider's handiwork
and she rebuilds and rebuilds.
Out of a cleft in the rock
the hand of a fig reaches outwards,
its five flat fingers, clawing for light,
sometimes waving mechanically, like a joke-hand.
Ignorant life it wants, its own kind of hale-and-heartiness.

What am I doing here? I do mean here,
doing something *here*. This ant on the page,
it is doing something, maybe trying to get off –
what is there in this snowfield for him after all?
So in that sense doing something,
I feel I ought to be doing when I'm here.

Is there something I can do for you?
Dead six months now and it is unbearable
to think all is discharged –
if my bit of the obsequies was done ok
is that it? Just to say
that what I am doing here is remembering you,
does that join the realm of acts
like giving money and digging wells
even if it's most like grave-tidying,
graves being things made for those who cannot care
for them, or notice them.
Graves, words (even graven words) always misaddressed,
the helplessness of remembering.
Another ant, another purpose for its tentative forefoot.
But I know you would not have me turn away.

' — is', is just to say, *that there* is
(the recourse to italics is regrettable,
survival of subject more compromising still)
and is, unpredicated, without profile, pronoun, names
or parts nothing outside, all things gathered in,
by thought and only by thought,
by the kind of mind we are –
and already I have said too much
and am tumbling into instances
as thought just as quickly disaggregates itself
into a day's worth of light,
the belly of an ant,
and other mortal things.

Can the universe become, no, I'll rephrase that,
is it — at heart — something like
the motion of bicycle wheels,
nothing of the tubing, leather, chrome, rubber
just the movement
can I ever see just the movement?
just the relay between wheel and wheel?

Is this idea ridiculous?
Is this a dangerous idea?

. There aren't many poems start this way,
but what I'm flagging is that there is always
something prior, something that has dwindled
or hung out, inexpressible or unspeakable,
some murmur-mutter before the throat-clearing.

So every start is in the smack and dab of things.
The conversation has been up and running so long
when I teeter in from a side road
on my velocipede it seems I can't keep up,
though no one's doing more than looking for clues,
looking at death from this side.

29

remembering the Pack Horse Hotel

Might I yet attain, at 65, with me old age pension,
me own ataraxy? Will I have earned it?
I'll make my case by saying I've never been one
to come on with 'some says one thing, some says another,
and who knows? And what's the odds?
Let's go down the pub.' I've sat in the pub,
and worried away (like Bertrand Russell sat in Whitehall
worrying away) highly engaged in argument,
sloshing beer on the barmaid's feet:
'God is dead. Long live the God that failed!'
'All hail the people's Bomb!' and other burdens.
And latterly, notebooks, full of it, worrying away.
So now, can I let me be?

The cherry tree does not worry away.
For all the ruffling and bending
of the daily wind it sways with calm.
It will not even mind its splintering,
which will come.
It does not even need to say
'Be as I am.'

Yet it is not: that is, it cannot be
in any way that we can think. It will not serve.

Ataraxy – A taxi – A tisket – A tasket –
always   whirr-whirring away

A sliver of red floor shows us just where in the room
his figures stand; behind them he paints the dust
hanging in the air. This is the spectacle of the world,
where it is his angels are
in the atomic swirl of an afternoon.
Piero knows that even he does not see everything,
this is just one of many seeings
and without shadow he would be blind.

31

after Gordon Matta Clark

He tears away the wallpaper and there is the street
fifty floors below, the carpet is sucked through the floor,
flapping downwards, snagging on plumbing pipes and ducts.
He exults: nothing is built but falls.
Laminates peel, cement perishes,
reinforcings poke through like fingers, buckle and rust.
Only in distress is art, he says,
Manhattan's coppery cliffs are sliding downwards,
crankshafts, old wheels, the guts of stoves are falling,
the plazas craze and flake into junkyards,
it's all a toy to take to bits.
The artist must not make but see what is hidden,
he says, breathe pure oxygen, what is always hidden,
he says.

sacking and gold: *sacco ed oro*

and be assured this is *not* the sun
you're looking at

this painter insists: do not look for the sun

I want my freedom and nothing I make
depends: tar is the stuff it is,
likewise pumice and Cellotex

and freedom must always be
vigilantly guarded

not for me a gas fire
and all that naked, scrotal love.

People get married now in aeroplanes
and the Pope has one of his own
and yet the world is still not modern!
Especially art, pottering in poppy fields and corn!

Now, circling over Verona, the arena tilts
this way then that, like a saucer,
so, see, there is no fixed point,
all is in motion and the view from here
'imposes a profound contempt for detail'.
Who cares for that man's tie, her scarf or skirt?
As it has always wished, the spirit soars from the earth,
our sculptures shall be mobile as the clouds,
cities burst upwards like chrysanthemums,
everything is dissolving into art!

34

I don't like Nature. I can try to though, and I do.
I look at it and after a while it does become
almost a landscape. There are green patches,
tawny patches, glassy patches,
and squinting I think I can make out
a small school of water-birds,
though they might be the much-relayed reflection
of houses near the shore. Do they move
or do they not? This is what exasperates me –
the anaemia – dots that might be birds' eyes
staring at me. I lose interest.
This grey cat is darker down the spine,
then faintly striped outwards –
But now that's pissed off leaving another blind spot,
another gobbet of it empty and un-understood –
like the two-tone jackdaw's cawing
as it visits and departs the apple tree.

The unicyclists on a tightrope are either
going at it *mano a mano* or jiving, it's hard to tell.
I hate Art. I can try not to, and I do, but to me it's like
climbing out through a difficult doorway in the rock
to meet what? Some light?
There might be a Chairman Mao
seen through a venetian blind – could be affecting –
and I am always taken by sand or chalk,
blown, poured or scattered on to adhesive
so that a childhood seems stuck there
in the glints and hillocks, the bits of the alphabet,
a piece of paste costume jewellery,
and now archaeology is necessary, geology even,
for this could be the Cretaceous of a life
I am entering, though it is hard to tell,
and what might be the right slippers or shoes?

If, after our ice-cream, we walked up some steps,
went inside and saw a photo of myself,
caught on a very good day, in just the right light
by that beautiful blonde photographer-mistress
(so it's said) to half the Rolling Stones,
blown up on a wall 10 feet high by 20 feet wide
with an invitation to the public to come and worship,
and Lila said 'Was that you, Grandpa?'
what would I make of it?
Did I ever recline just so?
Did I ever really meet a gaze as I met that lens?
And: how much do I love what once I was?

It can seem that I'm still what once I was,
struggling not to sniff, my finger in my eye.
But don't feel sorry, nor pause to imagine
major or minor shames, shallow cruelties
that I pray are now suppressed,
for these are not why I would want to turn away.
That surpasses even embarrassment,
the reason is just there in the steps of passing.

Schifano calls this painting 'sulla giusta soluzione
delle contradizioni in seno alla società'
which I will construe thus:
in seno, in the breast – we strike it here –
is where we feel for this as with the rising gorge,
the catch in the throat as we cry 'Justice! Justice!'
and have marched arm in arm;
and *in seno*, deep in the breast, deep in the heart,
wound as I imagine it, like the tightest, most intricate
serpent-coil, or the most intent spool, bobbin, armature,
lie the contradictions:
wealth is poverty but poverty is not wealth.

I would like to make a picture of the *giusta soluzione*
– what would it look like?

It will have to start with a line, in a circle,
and inside it I will draw me and mine.
But then the circle must be bigger
so I can accommodate you and yours,
and every detail of me and mine and you and yours
must be in accord so that I do not lavish
my attention on this vest, or that smile of mine, or yours.
But then the circle must be bigger
for the detail requires it and there is no reason
why those who are not me and mine or you and yours
should not be inside with us,
and I must attend to every eyebrow
and this is becoming back-breaking work,
even though all paintings are of something, not of everything.
But perhaps all of us can be symbolised,
say by a perpendicular and even stroke.
And now I can go on,
and the circle is become so wide none is outside
so there is no need of the line, or the stroke.
The picture is perfect. There is nothing there.

Space available. As my mind looks around
it sees a good deal: my love,
my great good fortune, my children,
my children's children. Then there is the lake
seen from above and the clouds' footfall upon it,
lifting, vanishing, resuming;
and the lake at my feet by the landing stage
with its arrhythmic slap-slapping
and its secret flowing away into the reeds.
This is not the complete picture of course.
Both lakes I am making stand in,
scribble-shading them to suggest happiness.
And there is, or, *but* there is, space available,
shapeless patches which if they are in the eye
must be in the mind, resolutely empty
of everything: lake-water, children laughing, even clouds.
I think they are the meadows of irreducible despair,
untenanted, but always to be kept aside.

quick quick quick quick quick quick quick quick
just the feet quick quick the shoes not court shoes
men's shoes office shoes immaculately laced-up shoes
the trouser turn-ups falling all but to the welt
nothing else visible the foot at its full angle back
each step reiterated quick quick quick quick
you want to join such a step everything
is in such a step the shoes will be shined
leather-soled and heeled not marching steps
not marching feet regular steps regular feet
the world wants to join such a step quick quick
quick quick quick quick quick

41

after Luca Fontana

I've remarked elsewhere on that razor-slash –
bold, vicious, into no more than canvas
but modelling for sure a greater anger
against all that presents, against all surfaces, all faces,
What is behind it? Black black black.

So it is a surprise to meet again
these punctures into the void
and see them now delicately cut,
even affectionately it seems,
small upturned isosceles, and so connected
they seem like lines of bunting,
no red white and blue, nor red white and green,
only grey, chalky white, the smears
of an accidental world and – how can it be? –
the little black flags,
nothing in themselves, but with a slight curl inwards,
are not so much baleful as jaunty.

I am I think indifferent to titles
but to be the Professor of Perspective,
how cool would that be!
The said Professor is said to have expired
crawling from his death-bed across the floor
towards the light as it split his shutter.
From the bed he would be in the middle ground,
the sun of course the vanishing point. Or could
the tumult of his sheets just be suggested
and he in the near foreground be reaching
towards where we, spectators, stand,
the light falling flat upon his face.
Given strength the Professor could have shuttled
among all such views as these, indeed chosen
every minute of the cardinal in turn to make a human view.
'The Sun is God,' he cried, but only the sun
sees the death-bed and the cry and everything
in heaven and earth in one single plane.

In none of the senses can this be art:
the Highway Surveyor's Department
has been along and spray-painted the roadway
with signs to mean 'dig here' ... 'amend' ...
'pipe' ... and through rain and shine
the codes lie weathering into the many greys
and granulations of asphalt. The road waits.

Until the painter happens by with his Polaroid.
He looks down. A car passes over. He blinks.
He blinks. A van. A bicycle. (For variation.)
He blinks again. They make no difference.
Home with his snaps he takes up his brush
and enters the marks, goes into them,
what other way is there to put it?
He enters the marks.
There is something else in there,
the road-code is a gift,
but there is something else in there
and only his brush can find it out.

44

'The Arrival of Implacable Gifts' is,
before it is anything else,
itself a wondrous gift.

Thank you too for your 'Sewing Circle'.
My notes wonder if these women are witches or Bretons,
and whether their dress-trains are trugs or cribs.
There is a child with tiny specs, I spot him.

But what have I missed?
My notes are not your picture.
Is that man being sewn into a tapestry Leonardo?
Near the seashore did I see shells
or peacock feathers, or shells
on peacock feathers?

Through such frail canals does one mind seek another.
The effort is the first thing I thank you for.

45

again after James Gleeson

And then you saw Italy!

Three cypresses and an umbrella pine,
the piazza a seashore where the boy David lies flat,
his head thrown back in a rockpool;
and the Madonna, in a private moment,
her blue gown thrown across her hips,
tends to her hair, and a hennaed girl,
wound in pearls and jewelled flowers,
floats on the waves from Africa.

And Man, who up in those flame-struck forests north
could not be the measure of Nature
but only part of its tumultuousness,
could be this boy in blue jeans,
jacket open, shirtless,
who has just crossed the unseen sound
and now, breaking the perspective,
berths his boat beside the colonnade.

You give me faith, my friend, you give me faith.

Grammatical am I, I now realise, am realising,
and since error always comes hard on the heels
of grammar, therefore I am already in error.
It is clear I do not know what I am saying.
I do not know what I am doing.
I do not know what I should do
but nonetheless I should be sure that
(I have heard this now many times)
I am acted and when I am done
I will have been passed through Nature
(a way of putting it I did not make
myself) as through a sentence, parole, parade.

'Inside' we say, or 'deep inside',
or '*in* my heart', or 'but with*in*
I feel ... the feeling persists'
'in here', and we strike our chest,
'here', he taps his chest, '*sono vecchio*',
this is where I am old,
this is where I was young
in here is where I am.

I'm on my way now.

I am at the lights, the crossing, School Lane,
better wait, I can't get these new switchings,
and this new phone.

Past there now. I've crossed over.
By the chip shop, well nearly.

You know I have to stop now.
The bridge is like a hill to me.
Is that how long I'm taking?
I'm doing as best I can.
No, don't fetch me.

Are you late? I'm sorry. Have you loaded the car?
I will be there, but I have lost this street.

I know I live near a tree.

49

Think of the crab's outrage when it insists
'I am not a crustacean
I am a crab, and myself.'

Likewise other creatures will not recognise themselves
among those typed by the Emperor;
or those who drink only from a china cup;
or those who once broke the moon.
Remember too the doughty penguin
never in troop with zebras, pandas and their like.

And how outraged are you, three years old today,
when you say 'I am not three, I'm four!'

Lucky fuck. That's me I mean. Fucking lucky
every which fucking way. Not a piece of my fucking life,
fucking definitely included, to fucking moan about.
Never fucked over at the proper or improper time
by melancholia, never dropped a buzz-saw
on my fucking leg, never told 'fuck off' by my kids
(fucking kids), no cancer or other fucker's worming
its way through my guts as best I know,
and 'Fuck the rich!' is ok by me 'cos I'm not
one of them, though I mustn't fucking grumble
and I don't, not fucking much.
Fuck me, what a life! Again, ah thanks.
Again? What a jousy and lucky fuck am I,
and I'd better fucking believe it.

A solitary walk by a riverside,

or starting early with my dog,

in either case *indulging a reverie*

though I know what *melancholy will attend*

since I would know and do not,

would be acquainted with

the nature and foundation of government, the principles of evil and of moral good, why I approve of one object and disapprove of another, call one thing beautiful and another deform'd? what are truth and falsehood, reason and folly? where am I? by a riverside or not? *or what? from what cause do I derive my existence, and to what condition shall I return? whose favour must I court and whose anger must I dread? what beings surround me and on whom do I have any influence, or who have any influence on me? the cause of these several passions and inclinations which govern me?* what is happiness? *how to decide 'twixt truth and falsehood, reason and folly*

WITHOUT KNOWING UPON WHAT PRINCIPLES I PROCEED

Oh *the dread of error, the absurdity of my reasoning*!
Some smudger with an easel and an oily thumb
can say 'there is nothing that is not a mystery to us',
I must prove Poor Reason. How can I live in mystery?

David Hume answers himself as for himself:

kick back and watch the Test or Tour all afternoon;
eat chocolate; take a front seat upstairs out
to the outskirts, the terminus and back, and back again;
josh with friends; take a glass or three; let reasoning slip
and pay no mind; and dunna worry yooth,
this is Nature helping you.

52

Believing ourselves monarchs,
what follows?

★

Those who put no stock in *maquillage*,
in pencilling, mascara, rouge or gel,
are they the blessed?

★

Those expert in their pencilling
because this is what they love
are they the honest ones?

★

Here's Pierrot in his knickerbocker suit of lights:
'this rich and spangled life
is given to us by life',
but who dares to be a clown?

★

Sometimes it happens that the way is beautiful,
like a single cloud.

★

Tomorrow it will be fine,
said the man clinging to the spar
'without a sight of land'.

★

On the street where you live
the solitary are always passing
and often halt.

★

The nobler the heart
the looser the collar.

★

No one believes
save in his own misery;
no one believes
save in his own deserving.

★

It is a hard horizon:
having been set to living,
at the end harder yet.

★

On your feet, dead men!
Stand up, stand up!

★

dura lex sed lex

'Inasmuch as life is *essentially* ... injuring ... oppressing...'
Ants die between pages, as no doubt in the sweeping of leaves,
and in the Tom Thumb floods of watering the lettuce.
The silhouette on the dyke in the middle distance
has the tread of a man. Were he content
to spend his days picking up stones or leaves,
bunching their stems into small bouquets
would this be a kind of the purest happiness?
There are many we know of, and who are loved,
so turbulent in mind, so injured and injuring
that this is all we can wish for them: life in itself.

They are always wise words those
Leonato says to Antonio, both *bravi*,
both old men but still learning the hard way
and Antonio especially willing to give contumely
what for – 'Come Signor Boy!' – and the words are:
'There was never yet philosopher
that could abide the toothache patiently.'

And it is what Melville says among the dunes to Hawthorne,
but then reports how sometimes he can lie on the ground
and feel as though his hair and fingers
are filaments of the grass,
each growing into each so that he knows himself
as part of what he must call the All –
for which there is no sound, not even the least sound.

But then sitting in those sands at Southport,
within the shades of the Customs House,
spear grass poking at the velveteen
and his hat always at risk from the breeze,
the world is back in its old divisions:
Melville and Hawthorne, Antonio and Leonato,
having to make again 'their push at chance and sufferance'
– 'Come Signor Boy, fight!'

Melville stretches on the sand.
Did he smoke cigars?
Did he keep a toothpick in his vest?

When he was in his All
what did he get out of it?

Fearlessness? Though not of the kind
born of his love of derring-do –
buccaneer, harpooneer, mountaineer –
but such that, were he picking his teeth of an evening,
leaning on his balcony rail,
and out of the clear sky
lightning found the metal that he held,
and were he granted an instant to think about it,
he would say and mean it: 'Death too is life.
I am absorbed, but nothing is unfinished.'

56

Strike through the mask! Strike through the mask!

Ay, ay Cap'n Ahab.
In some company imperatives are paramount:

Go be a wild man of the woods,
a wild man of the sea,
one of the great renouncers.

There where the mist steams off the hill
is where I want to be.
Let the cloud advance till I am cloud.

I hear of other modes of high indifference.

Can I imagine this?
I walk up to my enemy; I slice off my nose.
It lies at his feet. I slice off my left hand.
It drops to the ground. Is there blood in the dust?

Is there pain? If so it is felt.

Who feels it?

This question can't be understood.

Now, how did I intend to do that?

Did I say that I would do it?

By whom would I be understood?

'It was intended' is all that could be said.

But it must be understood.

The understanding is yet more important
than the sharpness of the blade.

There are those who have lived – and died – beyond enigma:
St Lawrence tucking his own gridiron under his arm;
St Agatha, coifed like Freya, imperturbable,
allowing a peek at her bleeding chest,
sometimes her paps held out in a dish;
Karl Liebknecht 'on leave from death'.
These are not more cases of the grand indifference
but some who just knew that this is only the first world,
fretted and sick, and another is, or will be – no matter which –
the good, better, best and real one.

Now, try all that again without
the ambush, be less arch.

It must be possible to tell a story.

A good man cannot be harmed.

The wall plaque reads:

Abitò qui, nel estate 1918,
il Beato Massimiliano Kolbe
che nel lager di Auschwitz
il 14 agosto 1941 offrì la sua vita
per salvare un padre di famiglia

Or in another version:

Here in the summer of 1918
lived the Blessed Massimiliano Kolbe
who in the lager at Auschwitz
on the 14th of August 1941
offered his own life
to save the father of a family.

It must be possible to tell a story.

A Fr. Kolbe (41) a Franciscan
was sent to Auschwitz
by the Germans for sheltering Jews
at his monastery in ...

A Fr. Kolbe (41) an anti-Semite,
as his writings show,
was sent to Auschwitz by the Nazis
for sheltering partisans ...

A Fr. Kolbe (41) was in Auschwitz
when one man escaped
and ten were picked
to die in his stead ...

A Fr. Kolbe (41) was in the line
but not picked out
when one of the ten,
a father ...

A Fr. Kolbe (41) heard
one of the men
cry out that he was
the father of a family ...

A Fr. Kolbe (41), hearing
one man plead for his life
and his children,
stepped forward in his place ...

A Fr. Kolbe (41) who had taken the place
of one Franciszek
Gajowniczek (46), was locked
with nine others ...

A Fr. Kolbe (41) who had taken the place
of a Jewish prisoner,
would die
of hunger and thirst ...

Saint Max, who is the subject
of my hero project,
led the prayers and singing
and amazed the guards ...

Saint Max, who I am
writing about for my project,
lived without any food or water
for three weeks ...

One Fr. Kolbe (41), still alive
ten days later when the cell
was needed, was killed
by lethal injection ...

Kolbe the anti-Semitic priest
is said to have taken the place of
Franz Gajowniczek
who was not a Jew ...

Fr. Kolbe was loved by all
the prisoners, and they reviled
the Jew Gajowniczek
who stood back and survived ...

Fr. Kolbe, still alive
when the cell was opened,
offered his arm to the doctor
for the carbolic acid ...

Fr. Kolbe was killed
by the usual drug employed,
phenol, injected by the medical staff
straight into the heart ...

It must be possible to tell a story.

'Let no man say he is happy until he is dead.'

When Kolbe stepped forward he defeated life,
and he knew he was a happy man.

Perhaps in his summer in Amelia in 1918
he stuck his nose into a dish of tomatoes
just from the stem and right into the stalks
and breathed and smiled and said
'This is life and this is good.'

And then he turned and went through a door
and stopped, as though looking for someone,
and then turned and went out again
and somewhere in this small confusion
put down the fruit and asked himself
'How may the heart be as good as this?
It also lives here.'

No answer spoke. But when he stepped forward
he knew he had learned to let life pass
and was a happy man.

But to be 'the father of a family',
this is life and this is good
and here life cannot pass
and this you clearly knew
as you stepped out to say 'Take me',
or words to that effect, or maybe
'This life is a thing for others.'

You must be understood.

Saint Maximilian Kolbe,
martyr for Charity not the Faith,
and contender for my hero project,
was this your stepping stone
to your better life
when at the last,
having no need of your spectacles,
you will climb naked
and perfectly toned
out of the manhole
the good doctor had
consigned you to,
or did you not see God at all,
only Franciszek Gajowniczek
who was either a Jew
or not a Jew and who cried
'What about my children?'
and who did or did not
do all right out of telling his story later,
and this was all you saw,
Franciszek or Franz, his flesh, his head,
the heads of his children,
and whether or not
you offered up your arm
or let the needle in
'twixt rib and rib,
you are telling me

'Be perfect as I am',
or, as I make you say:
'There is no thing cognisable
that says "Go do thou likewise",
and "A good man cannot be harmed",
there is only a human voice
to say it', as though
I could listen hard enough
to catch it.

58

'We are thus, we know not how.'

The frosted pancreas, even the just-subcutaneous,
harbour sometimes the silliest of worms,
the tiny bestial venoms that are of themselves –
ach! –
no wonder some of us are bound to hate
the snide, treacherous flesh: knuckles too wracked
to write a shopping list,
hate it for the shoes it makes us wear,
the callipers, for its instruction
that you can do nothing but fear
so that you want to say
'I am not this organity,
I am my Rational Soul,
that which is in me and without me
and will be after, or will not be after,
though how can I ever feel
how it had its living formerly
or entered?'

59

This poem is for all those who piss with pain.

But what it is not is a herbal whose good advice
to 'lay the leaves down' (steep them I assume)
should relieve 'them that pysse with payne',
for that must work. I do not offer 'work'.
Art is not a soup from marrow-bones,
afloat with greens, goodness and gratitude.
More humbly, I should say I *cannot* offer 'work'.
So what am I offering? (Art is always offering.)

I'll start with my dishonesty,
that though there was a true dedication (see above),
a call from strength to the sick and unlucky
whose world is next to mine,
as close as the universe of birds
and as separate,
what succeeds is simple selfishness,
the poem's own body trying on its gaudy,
and the call goes astray, thins out,
until they expect less, and less,
and then nothing of me
and my purposes.

60

Quixote's balsam, synthesised to cure every wound and ill,
produces only projectile vomiting
straight into Sancho's beard,
and breeches, pouched and dripping with shit.

Is this the Master's verdict,
not just on all daft worts and roots and spells
but on all remedy, all analgesic even,
for what is to be met along the road?

61

In the modern world, the urinal's periodic belch
brings back to mind the problems of life:
shit-handling in its many aspects;
catarrh in its various modes;
the arts of snot-handling in heavy weather;
flea-flapping; singeing the seams of shirts.

A man crapping,
crouching forwards, shirt-tails in the air,
pants round his skinny ankles,
knees out to open his bowels –
look, there's a levelling line there straight through
from arsehole to 'noble mind'.

But how easy this reduction,
how ready the belly laugh that *shit shit shit*
is this creature's true sum of reason –

how hard to eulogise
the so many Oddfellows,
the Sundays Dad gave for dying Billy Howes,
and those poor dear dead louse-hunters.

62

A man sits on a stool and sings. The people listen.
A butterfly settles on a flower
and someone, me perhaps, must see it,
but this is not the same kind of thing at all.
A man sits on a stool and sings, of love perhaps,
or of jasmine, or acanthus perhaps,
or of cafés deserted in the afternoons,
or of an old man he knew, a character to be sure,
or of a butterfly upon a flower,
and none of these is the same kind of thing as his song.
And the people, me among them, neither are we
the same kind of thing as his song, not at all,
and we listen as he sings.

I could get my kicks by dressing well.
I could tax the barber's craft at least fortnightly,
ask more of him than his cut-throat and cologne.
He would advise me on the bandaging
of my moustache and how it might decide
the all-important contour of my upper lip.
A boy's tremor would return to see the taper lit
and approach my nape-hair in his steady hand.

64

So Nature has a hidden order, the philosopher
or cosmologist can reveal. It has a tendency towards
concealment, a disinclination to show its hand
and the skeins of its web are thought all the stronger
half-disclosed, and its whole harmony —
could it be but sprung to view —
therefore shapelier and more certain sure.
Thus we are pinned, half-minds in a half-world
while everything around us is at work,
the banksia, or as it might be, miniature rose,
the near bodiless spider angling,
reflections bending inside bottle-glass.
If I close my eyes what do I see for myself?
a squareish red shadow shimmering in a shirt cuff.

65

I read the world for its hidden order.
In marriage guidance how are J & J
like A & B, and in turn like C & D, or E & F
and what will this yield for happiness?
The misery of such incongruities
haunts the counsellor
who must know cases but cannot seize
even the rough and readiness of cautious laws.
What gets said that destroys a mind for years
will be her province; the titrate of it
is stubborn, inscrutable and cruel.

'The hidden order' reprised – it never shows itself
and never goes away.
What? 'We should be content with chance not cause?'
What kind of talk is that?
Item: Doctor, this stuff you gave me –
for the eczema around my eyes?
a new thing to be turning up in my sixty-second year –
does work but it keeps coming back
and I want – sorry – I'd like to know why.
A late-developing latex allergy caught from
swimming goggles seemed very satisfactory,
and readily combatable, if the right ones can be found,
but experiment (no goggles, same rash) nixed that.
I'd like it to be like nicotine, the blue smoke seeps
and wreathes round my fingers and lo!
that sullen, browny, matt-finish yellow,
chemically so well understood.
But this is more like back pain,
except that really is something else:
lying down in a darkened room being fed
grants too much to the thought
that causality requires confusion, order disorder,
predictability – when it will recur – unpredictability.
Nothing hereabouts is really a joke.

The hidden *dis*order now, that is never hidden long.
The VAPE Dopopuntura (trademark registered),
works very well on insect bites – it's the ammonia –
but ammonia plus ice and you have
a chemical spill across the motorway,
quickly attended by jokes, confusion's close connivers
for whom skids are always funny, like bites:
Gnasher with a mouthful of trouser,
a bobby bemused by a wasp,
even crocs can be made to grin.
Monotheists convene in Madrid today to discuss
the human tragedy. Monotheists convene today
to discuss the human tragedy in Madrid.
'It's the way you tell 'em,' a hospital spokesman said.

Pagliaccio in a rented room, the landlord kindly,
and a tailor has made him an overcoat
of a weight and colour for autumn
and the food downstairs is as much and as good
as he can eat. Yet he bleach-cleans the lavatory
nine times a day, is never at the bidet
less than an hour, the skin round his arse,
the mortician will report,
is as red and rough as turkey-wattle.

Then a good friend seeks him out and they embrace,
laughing at the tears he's felt-tipped on his cheeks
till he again hurls himself on the divan
and his whole body starts and heaves.
Each night, the landlord says, he soft pedals
the piano, singing in his throat
that he is king of all the world,
a world that is new and will yet burst out.

In the 1950s when crêpe was new
and people stopped and stared
to watch the Teds slope past Dikiefido's,
the doggies in the window barking and jumping,
we all thought new imaginings of rubber
would change the world –
and plastic then was only just beginning.

1965. And thereabouts. Human nature was not
in question: it was good, at heart good,
if 'everywhere in chains', one chain being
'Human Nature' which would have us as
intractable as a fox when with one small
recalibration, tilt or nudge we would be shining.
So are we, in this air and light, almost alive,
or carboniferous, still waiting?

Thucydides, what would you say
if you could hear that I am tired,
tired of, don't believe in, broad horizons?
I can gaze all day at a shaftless garden fork,
heavy-brown with rust, useless, probably ugly,
but a thing that cleaves to me, is felt bodily,
as though it brings news
from the very bowels of truth.

Your war, Thucydides, was a very great war,
or it was not. It was complete and reasonable,
or a skirmish in the skirmishing.
What you ask is not that I steady myself
and hold the whole world in my head,
that might have been do-able.
No, what you ask is the understanding of it
once we are past cuticles and oxides.

Charlie had too many darlings and too many debts,
upped and went to Canada, not a dicky bird.
Until a card for his mother said he was in Liverpool,
on a troopship just landed. Then, not a dicky bird.

It is the Idea of History to see the categories of time,
and within the Idea are different ideas:
it is all a falling-away, a slow bully-roll downwards;
or it marches, always going up, always becoming, always not yet.

Charlie and his doxy, up the alleyway by the brewery, act.
Then, still in time, Charlie finds himself at
1st of July 1916, 07.30 hours, up with the lark.
Perhaps. Never a dicky bird.

73

'... survives first contact with the enemy'

such as those who came on bicycles
through the jungle
                and farewell the *Prince of Wales*
and my Uncle Percy, young blacksmith of Sandford Hill
whose easy sweetness in his photograph
has been with me all my days.
But would that I could have seen him move,
from the kitchen to a chair,
from the coalhouse to the fire;
to have heard him speak,
perhaps just reading the paper –
the loss of what I never knew has been with me
all my days, my mite of the world's wars'
deliverance. But nothing to his mother's,
sectioned for her grief,
locked in all that countryside
until she could say what he is now:
this photo, a frame of ordinary medals,
a stripe of wall, unvisitable,
where he is incised by race,
service-arm, rank, number, and alphabet,
in column 437, everything about him attended to daily
in this needful dream, this phantasm of order.

74

The liberty cap, ah, where did I put it
when I left to drink champagne?
Red as a coxcomb as he wore it
and I admired it,
and called him my *compagno*.

He snatched it from his head
and gave it me and walked on through the arch.
Either it had meant nothing,
an accidental purchase,
or else he knew the game was up
the moth had landed
and nothing strenuous would serve.

I kept it but where did I put it
when I left to drink champagne?

Diddle diddle dumpling my son Don
Went to bed with his trousers on,
One shoe off and one shoe on
Diddle diddle dumpling my son Don.

The Flagellator has one shoe off and one shoe on.
Is that for purchase as he lays into his work,
golf-swinging the scourge into enemy flesh,
or is it from a slip and stumble mishandling
the man to the whipping post?

Oh silly Don, as your mother sang,
struggling to learn your shoes,
going to bed with your trousers on – though you never –
and here you are again, one shoe off and one shoe on,
diddle diddle dumpling ...

76

The Flagellator, though once a baby
will never be depicted with a baby face.
Snag-toothed always, carbuncled,
no one ever loves a torturer,
not even one of our own.

And this is how we explain ourselves:
History gets him from his mother's lap,
where he implores and fits this to that,
and carves his education in the crafts of pain.
There is this actual world awaits,
its grammar is fixed and carries us to the end,
though itself it has no end,
and so are we absolved.

Swimming is the answer, notwithstanding Chairman Mao.
There, that strikes an attitude. What on earth
do I mean? Well, if water ever was our element
it is no longer, yet its foreignness feels welcoming.
It is the sense of suspension and of clothing
at its simplest and most complete.
Admittedly it is escape, nothing to do with here above
except for drawing off the empty air – and maybe
it is blameworthy to embrace such muffling,
such coddling, which brings me on to Chairman Mao,
the Great Unmuffler, Pilot of Reality
for whom the world was full of answers,
one such that swimming is resurrection:
'You thought me dead? Look, seven miles
down the Yangtse, pick the bones out of that.'
But was he swimming or did he just float downstream?
Was that indeed his head singing? Hence the 'notwithstanding',
that and the bones.

78

How much impartiality should we try for?
We look up for an answer? Up.
Down. Straight ahead.
The floaters are stirred up
like the flakes in a snow-globe
Blackpool tower in a white-out.
Blink. Blink and blink again.
Slowly it settles and the viewing platform
returns to view.

And somewhere everything is understood.
Up there – that is the old idea, as frescoed,
and this is the new idea:
the hot news from the ice-cores;
the definitive history
of the Hong Kong and Shanghai Banking Corporation;
every lairage docket ever filed.
These are what move me hither and thither, impartially.

History could make a stone weep

John, what takes you back to Evensong so late?
Did History fail you?

I, who have spent no time at all in archives or the field,
have to say it is still the Book of Where Things Happen,
The Book Endlessly Corrected, the Book of Witness,
The Book of Expectant Understanding.
It absorbs us and it should.

★

When Deian's mobile went off
I heard you guffaw from the coffin.
That's a fact. No it's not. Who else heard it?
But how much impartiality should we try for?
I'm talking *to* you John, not 'for' you …

… sometimes in 'conversational French':
… *le grand vin blanc de Bourgogne … la grammaire
des civilisations …* how *actuel* is
le monde actuel? … does it just roll through us,
and by the by absolve us from any blame attached?
How much impartiality should we try for?

★

Surprising you in the backmost pew,
I'm curious to know if it be the music or the words?
Can I catch you murmuring *Now lettest Thou …* ?

Thou of whom it is said: *Thou* knowest all things,
Of whom it is said: *Thou* canst do all things
Of whom it is said: is in all things just
Who will grant us grace

because we find we are not
and cannot do these things

as History shows

and need these things

as History shows

at least to imagine them

as History shows.

And we are not absolved.

★

John, reason with me,
am I hearing you aright?

I meditate before a smeary window now,
dried rivulets between the panes,
small moraines where the runnels halted,
not quite randomised.

Apparently it can be known who I am
by the particular way I sneeze.

Like with a sermon in a high wind
it becomes uncertain who is speaking to whom.
My friends, I am doing my best to find
what it is I have to say,
but I end up shrugging at the street corner.

Of course others will break in,
and so they should, they have every appearance
of entitlement.
Others will be murmuring together,
as though making some necessary plan
and are clustered across the road, heads together,
glancing over their shoulders
and something of what they say carries here.

Lady, he does not like your briefcase or your shoes,
nor for certain the London train,
it is all 'darksome clay' to him,
denizen of the underpass,
who must like its wet floor, dark stones,
who must hate all things white, even if they are
'least complicated', 'easiest to understand'
'most pure':

No hurry Lady, clicky-clacky, clicky-clacky
There is no fuckin' place to go
We're only going to the crem.

83

The soul, I'm finding, turns out very useful.
If we have just the world as it is to go on,
how it wags, or its history seen
from any partiality whatsoever,
we'd think *è fango il mondo,*
what a shithole!

But in the dimple, mortise, sinus or grot
that gets called 'soul',
which is always *in in in,*
is, for instance, what gets called 'justice'.
Out here she can barely dress herself, go out
and be recognised – and she must be recognised
and face down those who say
'Who are you?' or 'Where have you ever been?'
or 'We have long forgotten you, we do pretty much
what we like', and she must skulk and bide
and her place of biding in this meanwhile,
this useful soul.

Meanwhile, a challenge: find me one person
in any bus queue, or indeed anywhere
who will deny that there's injustice
in this whole wide world of freedoms
and indulgences. Not one. I thought so.
The queue smiles ruefully and soldiers on.
So, Justice, how are you forgotten?
How are you whittled and distracted?

Philosophers, divines, all you addicts of good news,
sweet or sweating on the Ideal Power,
you will insist Injustice sits only on a paper throne
forever jumping and starting fearful of a spark,
spooked by a wall, a shadow, a creaking door.
In that case where is the ghost?
I cannot see the ghost.

Judge of the world am I. *La vita è bella*
or *la vita è brutta*? It's for me to decide.
Which network and which payment-plan?
Cool. How should I set to work?
The task is to gather up for contemplation
and assize every hair that will testify
to the joy and beauty of the life
we mortals lead, then put in litigation
every smudge upon the scene.
The rules of evidence must ban the ping-pong
of examples, smiley faces versus amputees.
Synechdoche is opportunist, often cruel.
Ciao bella. Ciao brutta. The court will rise.

87

In portraiture, what I favour for myself
is that nineteenth-into-twentieth-century
seaside look. *A bas* the aldermanic,
fists closed over the lion-carved chair-arms,
calf-bound History and Law behind,
frozen for the flash.
I want something more *Le Touquet Plage*,
dashed off, *impressioniste*, as though my laughing mistress
is just out of frame or shot and I am eager
to be off. Or even the style of collier lads
on the Isle of Man with their canes, boaters
and blazers plucked from the props box.
Not that I despise the aldermen who build and serve –
but oh, white sand, white flannels, something sunshiny.

Generous as it is, loving indeed to many,
the mathematics cannot help. There's a bumble-buzz
from the listening devices but nothing parsable;
from the ooze the odd statuette
brought up with the abalone is not germane;
naught from the geological squires;
nothing even from Darwin's beloved stenches.
For all-of-it-together, common-or-garden
taken-for-granted Being, for the universe –
whatever that is – nothing speaks.

So we are left to our own intricacies,
gli animali parlanti, the speaking clocks,
yapping at the Giant's castanets
like dogs to a bagpipe,
some of us stomped, some of us squeaking free
only to fall into allegories like this of
Human Ignorance where *Virtus Humana*, poor lamb,
has changed herself into a tree
she's that pissed off, and there we all are
down in the *fosse*, the pit, the maggot tin
and there's only Hermes (why Hermes?)
lending a hand to grasp and pull by one arm – who? –

Some who might yet try to find joy in the found,
like Whitman on his walks smiling at every sparrow,
though now bits of metal, half-beams,
rope both whole and unstrung, human things,
pieces that can be drop-soldered into non-machines,
tiny or bus-sized with such elaborate juncturing
and levering. Meanwhile the patient louse
ports its carapace across the speckled stone.
It is no model though, and no way to end,
not even this part of the conversation.

89

Like many others of my ilk this is not something
I like to talk about, but since, despite everything,
it still makes sense to talk of –
oh, wait, in my notes 'talk' is crossed out
and replaced by 'think' –
since it still makes sense to think of G—d
(as my religious students always write it)
especially, as I now have a philosopher's warrant
that s/he could be described by any analogy,
anything could be slotted into the sentence –
'father' (usually) 'watchmaker' (several times), 'spider'
or 'A' 'AA' or 'AAA', Adidas, *ad infinitum*,
it still makes sense because something must go just there
in such sentences that we do need like:
' — knows', ' — is good', ' — is just'
' — watches', ' — loves (me)', ' — is'.

90

So, I say *so*, if what G—d is is an unavoidable way of talking:
when everything has been imagined,
at least until everything is spoken whereof we cannot speak –
how many such sentences should we try for?

'G—d knows' let us take; and unpack:

day

Should lose his light when men do lose their shames,
Betray their cause of being

'G—d knows' *our cause of being* which is:

since we have a brain of a kind

can recognise the shapes and some shadows

of this world, in other words we can think –

G—d knows we can think! –

our cause is to think together,

one of another, and that must secure us here

and then comfort us somehow.

So, a first sentence can be: G—d loves Reason.

On my veranda I have to imagine more.
Sometimes, even on an easy day, it is difficult;
sometimes things can come unbidden, as they should:
a calabash of babies' hands rests in the hearth,
the little amputees themselves are who knows where.

Will it help to study more? Certainly.
And we have sought fore and aft, hither and yon,
up hill and down dale – we human things will not rest
until we know that the peace is within us
as once it was, and unabashed as once it was –
we *must* return. Or we might be new,
straightened at least, even refigured,
not quickly, but as we shall need to be.

I am always on the lookout for routines
and perhaps I can make another out of what I'm doing now.
I have woken early and stayed put.
Behind the shutters it is dark so what we call the day
is beginning only in noises: birdsong obviously,
which is at present an eight-call sequence
gargling in a pigeon's throat; other note-rows are
too fast to count. There are trees in a light wind,
a thousand leaves perhaps, and I realise
I have never thought to wonder how many leaves
a given tree might carry on a given day –
not a routine. A car starts and idles,
the driver checks her bag for tissues and for keys,
and further off – light is coming in now – a dull then whining pitch
resolves itself into a wood-saw. Whoever works it,
already stripped to the waist, is properly guarded I hope,
and alert. And little of this, really, is what I hear,
and what would the routine accomplish? Haphazard
attention? Exercise for the inner eye?
Let it be itself (reason enough for routines?)
A wasp is buzzing by the wall.
There are, I'm convinced again, surrounding worlds.

A lawyer on the beach,
jacketless, but still with my thin bow tie
in place, my pencil-moustache not yet
glistening and though my nose is reddening
I look straight at you, the viewer,
client, adversary – whoever you are.
'The nobler the heart the looser the collar'?
No, I don't entertain that.
Over my right shoulder a noonday light
is merging my shirt and the empty sand,
my outline is becoming all but lost.
Will this make you warm to me?
I feel sure in my eye there is a twinkle to be seen.

May the barber find happiness with his bearded lady.
May the wife who found her husband hanging
and tried to cut him down find a good companion
and stroll and kiss in the starlight.
May the slow one, the lame one, the ugly one
always be as welcome among the girls.
May she who never rests, who walks in the same street
all day every day with just a cigarette, find rest.
May she who grieves – he left after lunch,
at 3 he lay crushed in the field –
smile at one small thing and at length at another.
May there be dancing in the piazza!
May there be fruit upon the vine (literally).
For this is not a wicked but a hard world,
and people struggle, without a scheme of things,
and deserve release. That's it, willing it so.

There is the world we die in and there is nothing.
The shades know this, hence their clamouring,
which we learn to turn from, and which fades away.
Despite appearances, the gardens of remembrance
are full of resignation. 'At rest', they rest.
We stop by but are ushered on our way.
If we did not act as though this were true
what would become of us?

*

There is the world we die in and there is
somewhere we cannot visit, still less lodge in,
and we call it Truth.
(Do not be embarrassed to name it;
the hostess is a worthy lady
of impeccable, that is to say of course
no parentage, nude and desirable,
nude and pure as the sky, though, in a word, untouchable.)
It we did not act as though this were true
what would become of us?

Acknowledgements and Notes

Acknowledgements

Special thanks for discussion and encouragement to Judith Wainwright, Shirley Chew, Jon Glover, Rachel Mann, John McAuliffe, Helen Tookey, John Whale; to Michael Schmidt, Judith Willson, Eleanor Crawforth and all at Carcanet; to Leonid Lerman for his generous permission for use of the cover image, and to Elizabeth Cook and Helen Tookey for permission to use quotations in the epigraphs.

*

Several parts of *The Reasoner* have previously appeared elsewhere under different titles. I am grateful to the editors of the following publications:

American Poetry Review; *Eyewear* (toddswift.blogspot.com); *The Manchester Review* (www.the manchesterreview.co.uk); *Moving Worlds*; *The North*; *PN Review*; *Poetry & Audience*; *Revista Canarias de Estudios Ingleses*, no. 60, 2010 (Universidad de La Laguna); *Revue LISA / LISA e-journal* (Littératures, histoires des Idées, Sociétés du monde Anglophone), vol. 7, no. 3, 2009, Festschrift honouring René Gallet (www.lisa.revues.org/72); *Stand*; *The Wolf*.

Notes

The following notes acknowledge the sources of direct or adapted quotations that appear in the poems.

4–8 'Is our language complete?': '… ask yourself whether our language is complete', Ludwig Wittgenstein, *Philosophical Investigations*, trans. G.E.M. Anscombe (1953; 2001), no. 18.

29 'me own ataraxy'; after *ataraxia*: state of tranquillity free of all disturbance, as achieved by Epicurean philosophy; Samuel Beckett, *Molloy* (1979), p. 40: '… I grew calm again and was restored, in the face of nature's pranks, to my old ataraxy, for what it was worth.'

44–5   After two paintings by the Australian artist James Gleeson (1915–2008).

51   'the nature and foundation of government ...': David Hume, *A Treatise of Human Nature* (1739), Book I, 'Of the Understanding', section VII.

52   After some of the prints in the series *Miserere* by Georges Rouault (1871–1958).

53   'Inasmuch as life ...': 'To talk of intrinsic right and wrong is absolutely nonsensical: intrinsically, an injury, an oppression, an exploitation, an annihilation can be nothing wrong, in as much as life is *essentially* ... something which functions by injuring, oppressing, exploiting, and annihilating, and is absolutely incomprehensible without such a character', Friedrich Nietzsche, *The Genealogy of Morals* (1887), quoted by Philippa Foot, *Natural Goodness* (2001), p. 110.

79   'History could make a stone weep', Marilynne Robinson, *Gilead* (2004), p 216. 'Human beings do not make history ... Rather it is history that makes human beings and thereby absolves them from blame', Fernand Braudel, *A History of Civilisations*, quoted by Albert Manguel, review in the *Independent*, 6 March 1994.